DATE

# Cornerstones of Freedom

## The Story of

# THE MONITOR AND THE MERRIMAC

By R. Conrad Stein

Illustrated by Keith Neely

 CHILDRENS PRESS, CHICAGO

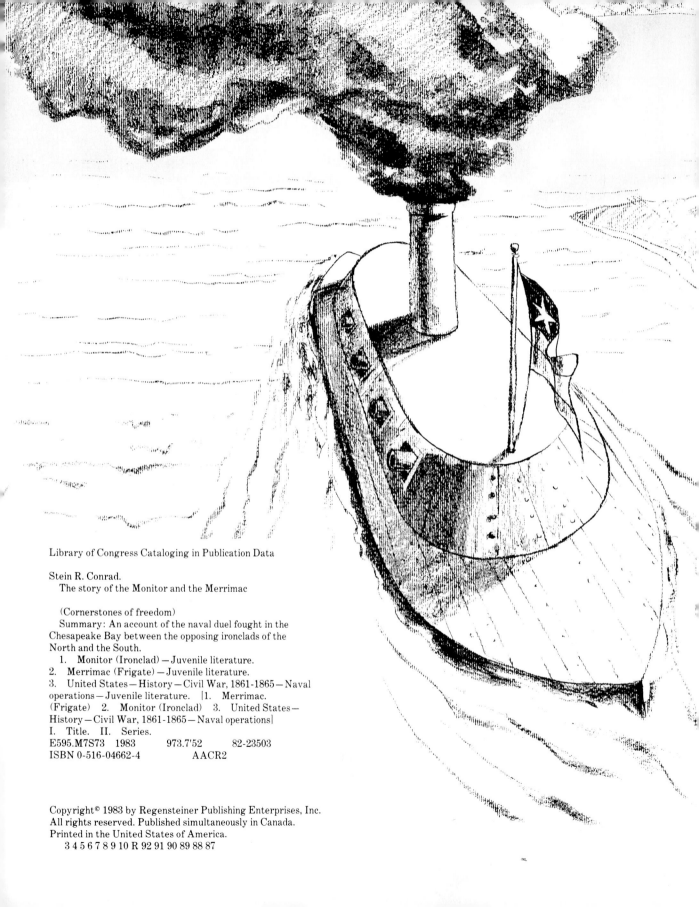

Library of Congress Cataloging in Publication Data

Stein R. Conrad.
 The story of the Monitor and the Merrimac

 (Cornerstones of freedom)
 Summary: An account of the naval duel fought in the
Chesapeake Bay between the opposing ironclads of the
North and the South.
 1.  Monitor (Ironclad) — Juvenile literature.
2.  Merrimac (Frigate) — Juvenile literature.
3.  United States — History — Civil War, 1861-1865 — Naval
operations — Juvenile literature.  [1.  Merrimac.
(Frigate) 2.  Monitor (Ironclad) 3.  United States —
History — Civil War, 1861-1865 — Naval operations]
I.  Title.  II.  Series.
E595.M7S73 1983      973.7'52      82-23503
ISBN 0-516-04662-4          AACR2

By March 8, 1862, the American Civil War had been raging for nearly a year. That spring morning a new and puzzling Confederate ship steamed up the Elizabeth River in Virginia. The Northern forces had a stronger navy than had the South. Union ships were blockading Confederate ports to cut off trade. The South hoped its new ship would be able to blast the Northern fleet out of the water.

The Southern ship was an ironclad. Once she entered battle, naval history changed forever.

Warships with iron armor built above their decks were not invented in the United States. Both the British and French navies had commissioned ironclads even before the American Civil War began. But those European ships had never seen battle. The first combat between armored vessels would take place in America.

The warship built by the South was called the *Virginia*. Some witnesses claimed she looked like a "floating barn roof." Her bottom was made of oak.

5

But rising above her decks were slanting iron walls that measured three inches thick. Poking through portholes in the walls were eight cannon—four on each side. The ship also had a bow gun and a stern gun. Finally, an arrow-shaped ram jutted from her bow like a huge iron beak. Surely the *Virginia* looked like a metal monster.

The *Virginia* had been converted from a wooden steamer. It had taken fifteen hundred men ten months of furious work to turn her into an ironclad warship. The wooden steamer had been called the *Merrimac.* Over the years, most historians continued to call the Southern ironclad the *Merrimac,* not the *Virginia* as the Confederates had renamed her.

As the *Merrimac* churned up the Elizabeth River, thousands of curious civilians gathered on the banks to watch. The civilians were Southerners. Most of them cheered the Confederate warship. But a *Merrimac* sailor named Hardin Littlepage wrote: "One man, I remember later, called out to us, 'Go on with your old metallic coffin! She will never amount to anything else.'"

Perhaps many of the sailors thought of the *Merrimac* as their coffin. The heat inside her was almost

unbearable. A sailor named Keeler complained, [We were] "broiling in our iron box." She was also a top-heavy, clumsy craft that could steam no faster than five miles an hour. Her engineer said, "She steered so badly that. . . it took from thirty to forty minutes to turn." The tremendous weight of Merrimac's armor forced the ship to ride dangerously low in the water. If she ventured into shallow water, she could get stuck in mud or her wooden bottom could be ripped to shreds on rocks. At sea, even a mild storm could sink her.

But in battle, *Merrimac*'s thick armored sides would protect her crew from enemy shells. Still, no one could be certain how an ironclad would perform in combat. Armored vessels had yet to be tested.

Ahead of the *Merrimac* drifted the Union warships *Congress* and *Cumberland.* Both were wooden vessels with tall masts and sails. They were part of a flotilla of Northern ships that had been tying up Confederate shipping in Chesapeake Bay for months. The two ships drifted at anchor just three hundred yards from the port city of Newport News. Their sails drooped and crewmen's clothing hung out to dry on the ship's line. An officer on board the *Merrimac* later wrote, "Nothing indicated that we were expected."

But the Union navy knew the Confederates had
been building an ironclad. Wild stories about its
might had spread from ship to ship. The Northern
sailors wondered which of their ships would be first
to tangle with the iron beast.

The huge *Merrimac* was quickly spotted by
lookouts on the two Union warships. On the decks of
the *Cumberland* and *Congress*, drummers beat a
rat-a-tat alarm. Some sailors scurried up the rig-
ging to untie sails. Others covered the decks with

sand. The men shuddered as they saw the sand being spread. It was meant to soak up blood from the dead and wounded so that men firing the cannons would not slip on the deck.

When the black iron *Merrimac* churned closer, many Union sailors dropped their work and stood frozen in astonishment. Never before had they seen such a ship. "As she came ploughing through the water right toward our port bow, she looked like a half-submerged crocodile," wrote Lieutenant A. B. Smith of the *Cumberland*. "I could see the iron ram projecting, straight forward, somewhat above the water's edge."

The world's first battle pitting iron against wooden ships would soon begin.

Confederate Captain Franklin Buchanan pointed the *Merrimac* directly at the *Cumberland*. He was determined to use the 1500-pound ram attached to the bow of his ship. The ironclad's advance brought her within range of the Union warship *Congress*.

The *Congress* opened fire with a broadside of twenty guns. A dozen shells hit squarely on the side of the metal giant. But they bounced harmlessly off her thick hide. Then the *Merrimac* fired her own broadside at the *Congress*. The shells ripped into her wooden enemy. "All I remember about that broadside," wrote a sailor on the *Congress*, "was of feeling something warm, and the next instant I found myself lying on the deck beside a number of my shipmates."

On the *Cumberland*, gunners worked like machines. They fired shell after shell at the oncoming *Merrimac*. But, Lieutanant A. B. Smith later said, they could see their shells "bouncing upon her mailed sides like India rubber, apparently making not the least impression."

At the range of fifty yards, the *Merrimac* fired her own bow gun at the *Cumberland*. The shell screamed into one side of the wooden ship and out the other. That first hit killed at least nine crewmen. Again and again *Merrimac*'s bow gun pumped shells into the *Cumberland*. At the same time, the giant ironclad inched steadily closer to her enemy. Finally, the *Merrimac*'s bow crashed into the *Cumberland*'s side. The ironclad's half-submerged ram pierced the wooden ship like a huge iron spear. Lieutenant Minor of the *Merrimac* claimed, "The crash into the *Cumberland* was terrific in its results. . . . Our cleaver fairly opened its side." Another *Merrimac* sailor said the ramming left a

hole in the *Cumberland* big enough to "drive in a horse and a cart."

After the collision, Buchanan ordered his engineer to reverse engines. While backing out, the massive iron ram dislodged from *Merrimac*'s bow and remained stuck in the side of the *Cumberland*. The loss of that arrow-shaped ram would be vitally important the next day when *Merrimac* was to fight the battle of her life.

The crippled *Cumberland* now drifted helplessly. Still her captain refused to surrender. Buchanan pivoted the *Merrimac* and began to pound the *Cumberland* with broadsides. Aboard the *Cumberland*, Lieutenant Stuyvesant claimed he saw "a scene of carnage and destruction never to be recalled without horror.... The once clean and beautiful deck was slippery with blood, blackened with powder, and looked like a slaughterhouse." Finally, the *Cumberland* sank like a stone. Many of the wounded who were unable to swim went to the bottom with her. The ship's chaplain also drowned. He was last seen kneeling on the deck praying for the souls of the many dead crewmen.

Captain Buchanan next wheeled his ironclad into a long, lazy turn and headed for the fifty-gun warship *Congress*. During the battle, the *Congress* had pasted the Southern ironclad with shells. But they had been like mosquito stings to the iron beast. Now, afraid of being rammed, the captain of the *Congress* steered his ship into shallow water where the low-riding *Merrimac* could not follow. It was a wise move, but the *Congress* could not escape the *Merrimac*'s guns. Buchanan stayed in deep water and raked his enemy with shellfire. *Merrimac*'s guns fired both solid shots and the newly developed exploding shells. The exploding shells hit their target, penetrated, and then blew up. Exploding shells could quickly turn wooden warships into matchsticks.

The decks of the *Congress* became a nightmare. The twisted bodies of dead crewmen lay strewn about. Blood soaked the deck. A fire roared in the hold. Finally, a shell fragment killed the ship's captain. The junior officer decided to stop the slaughter and surrender his ship. Later that night, the burning warship exploded and sank.

Two other Union ships, the *Roanoke* and the *Minnesota,* tried to join the fight. But while racing to the battle site, the steam-powered *Minnesota* ran aground. She became hopelessly stuck in the mud near the town of Hampton Roads, Virginia. While stuck fast, she would be an easy target. But there were problems on board the *Merrimac,* too. Captain Buchanan had left the inside of his iron ship to supervise the evacuation of Union sailors from the burning *Congress.* While standing on the deck, he was hit and seriously wounded by a rifle bullet. Command of the *Merrimac* passed to a young lieutenant named Catesby Jones. Dusk was approaching

and Jones decided to order the *Merrimac* back to the Elizabeth River.

The first battle between iron and wooden ships had been witnessed by thousands of people. Many had watched from the shore and others saw the fight from dozens of small boats that milled about Chesapeake Bay. Everyone viewing the melee knew that an era had ended. For centuries, wooden warships had ruled the oceans. Now it was certain that a single ironclad could destroy a whole fleet of wooden ships. In one afternoon, two thousand years of naval warfare had become obsolete.

Aboard the *Merrimac,* a very satisfied Lieutenant Minor wrote, "The IRON and HEAVY GUNS did the work. It was a great victory."

Indeed, the sinking of two Union warships was a great victory for the South. But the Northern forces also had been building an ironclad ship. At the same time the *Merrimac* was destroying the Union's wooden ships, the Northern ironclad was being towed down the Atlantic toward Chesapeake Bay. The next day, the two metal monsters would meet and fight a duel that would shake the world.

The Union ironclad was called the *Monitor.* It was the creation of an inventive genius named John Ericsson.

Ericsson was an engineer who had been born in Sweden. His earlier inventions included the first steam-powered fire engine and a screw-type propeller for ships. In 1841, Ericsson came to America. There he drew up plans for an ironclad warship whose guns would be housed in a spinning turret. At first, Ericsson tried to sell his design to Napoleon III, emperor of France. But the French leader showed little interest. When the American Civil War broke out, the North learned that the South was building an ironclad ship. The Northern leader,

Abraham Lincoln, was shown a cardboard model of the ship Ericsson wanted to build. It is reported that President Lincoln saw the model and said, "All I can say is what the girl said when she put her foot in the stocking. 'It strikes me there's something in it.' "

Lincoln ordered Northern shipyards to build Ericsson's ironclad as quickly as possible.

Rising from the *Monitor's* deck was a radical new gun turret. Older warships had guns that pointed out of their sides. Those guns could be turned only a few degrees to the left or right. In order to strike another ship, a captain had to aim his vessel's broadside at the enemy. But the *Monitor's* two guns were housed inside a turret that was driven by a motor. It could swing around like a merry-go-round. The swinging turret allowed a captain to aim his guns at an enemy regardless of the position of his ship. Never before had a warship with such a turret entered battle.

In both the North and the South, newspapers printed stories of the overwhelming damage inflicted by the *Merrimac* on her wooden opponents. Some Southern newspapers predicted that the ironclad eventually would send every ship in the Union navy to the bottom. Other papers claimed

that the *Merrimac* would steam up the Potomac River and shell the city of Washington. Still others said the "floating fortress" would lead Southern armies to the capture of Philadelphia, New York, and Boston.

Aboard the *Merrimac*, Lieutenant Jones had less-ambitious plans. His first goal was to destroy the *Minnesota*, which was still stuck in the mud near the town of Hampton Roads.

On the morning of March 9, 1862, the *Merrimac* steamed out of the Elizabeth River. A pillar of black smoke belched from her stacks. Accompanying the ironclad were several smaller Confederate ships. As the flotilla broke into open water, the Confederates were astonished by what they saw. A strange-looking new ship drifted just a stone's throw from the *Minnesota*. "Such a craft as the eyes of a seaman never looked on before," wrote Confederate Lieutenant James Rochelle, "an immense shingle floating in the water, with a gigantic cheesebox rising from its center. . . . What could it be?"

It was the Northern warship *Monitor*. Like the cavalry in the old western movies, the Union ironclad had arrived just in time to stop a massacre. The sea battle of the century was about to begin.

Like prehistoric dinosaurs, the two ironclads drifted silently toward each other. Then they paused, as if wondering which of them would make the first move. Behind the two ironclads rose the sails of the grounded *Minnesota*. Commanding the *Monitor* was Lieutenant John Worden. His orders were to protect the immobile warship.

Thousands of people watched from the shore and from small boats. From a distance, the two ships about to do battle must have resembled David and Goliath. The Northern *Monitor* seemed tiny compared to the Southern *Merrimac*. The *Merrimac*'s slanting iron walls towered above the Union ship. The Southern ironclad was about the length of a football field. The Northern ship was only three-quarters that length. And the *Merrimac* weighed more than twice as much as the *Monitor*. One Northern sailor later confessed, "to tell the truth, we did not have much faith in the *Monitor*."

Historians disagree as to which ironclad fired the first shot. But just four days after the battle, Lieutenant Greene of the *Monitor* wrote a long letter to his mother. In it he said: "As the *Merrimac* came closer, the captain passed the word to commence firing. I triced up the port, ran the gun out,

and fired the first gun; and thus commenced the great battle between the *Monitor* and the *Merrimac*."

With a roar of thunder, the two ships hurled shells at each other. Sometimes the ironclads disappeared under clouds of white smoke that puffed out of their cannons. During most of the battle they fought within fifty yards of each other. Spectators counted five times when the two ships actually touched.

The captains quickly learned that the *Monitor*, despite its size, had some advantages. *Monitor*'s deck rose only two feet above water level, making her a difficult target to hit. Also, the *Monitor* could steam at seven miles per hour compared with the *Merrimac*'s five. Finally, the *Monitor* had the revolutionary swinging turret. Confederate sailors were stunned when they saw the huge turret swivel to the left or to the right, stop, and bark out shells.

"You can see surprise on a ship just as you can see it in a human being," wrote a *Monitor* seaman named Truscott, "and there was surprise all over the *Merrimac*."

The *Monitor*'s shells did hit the *Merrimac*, but the iron giant remained unharmed. The *Monitor*, too, when hit, shed shells as if they were rubber balls.

During battle, the two ironclads sometimes looked as if they were locked in a macabre dance. The speedier *Monitor* sailed in circles around the *Merrimac* as she tried to get a shot at her bow or stern. In turn, the *Merrimac* pivoted clumsily as she tried to train all four of her broadside guns on the *Monitor*. The music for this waltz of the ironclads came from the ships' guns, which thundered like the devil's own drumbeats.

Like most battles, this duel in Chesapeake Bay was confusing. The two ironclads fought almost in the shadow of the grounded warship *Minnesota*. At times, the *Merrimac* found itself battling both the iron *Monitor* and the wooden *Minnesota*. At one point, the *Monitor* had to withdraw to hoist more shells into her turret section. Then the *Merrimac* and the *Minnesota* faced each other. The *Minnesota* was one of the most powerful wooden battleships on earth. She hit the Southern ironclad with an enormous broadside that included two ten-inch guns, fourteen nine-inchers, and seven eight-inchers. According to Captain Van Brunt of the *Minnesota*, that much firepower would have "blasted any wooden ship in the world out of the water." But the shell hits produced only a few dents on the *Merrimac*.

Even though the sailors inside the iron ships seemed safe from cannon fire, they were suffering. Above them, the sun beat down on black iron roofs. From the engine room, coal fires roared and high-pressure steam gushed through pipes. On both ships the inside temperatures rose to 140 degrees Fahrenheit. Crews manning the guns stripped themselves practically naked. Gunpowder blackened

their bodies. One sailor later wrote that the men had "perspiration falling from them like rain."

In addition to the ovenlike heat, an avalanche of noise tormented the crewmen. Belowdecks, machinery ground, steam sizzled, and pumps pounded. Each time a cannon fired, the explosion made the iron walls ring an earsplitting note. And when an opponent's shell hit the outside armor, it sounded as if a giant had struck the vessel with a sledge hammer. "The din inside the turret was terrific," wrote seaman Truscott of the *Monitor*. "The sound of every solid ball that hit fell upon our ears with a crash that deafened us." Once Truscott made the mistake of leaning against the iron wall inside *Monitor*'s turret. Suddenly a cannonball struck the outside wall inches from his head. "I dropped like a dead man," wrote Truscott. He was carried to sick bay with blood flowing from his ears. Seaman Truscott was unconscious for more than an hour, but he recovered.

Somehow the sailors suffered through the awful heat, the clang of shells, and the choking smoke of gunpowder. Furiously, the iron monsters continued to blast each other with their cannons. But, like two crayfish fighting in a jar, neither could damage the other.

Then the *Merrimac* sailed into disaster. The heavy ship, riding low in the water, ran aground. At once, Lieutenant Worden of the *Monitor* realized his enemy was stuck in the mud. Skillfully he positioned his ship at the stern of the *Merrimac*, where his opponent's broadside guns could not hit him. At close range, Worden fired at the helpless *Merrimac* with both his guns.

Inside the *Merrimac* the men worked frantically to free their ship from the mud. The ship needed more power to break loose. Crewmen threw wood, cotton, and rags soaked with turpentine into the furnace. As the fire roared, the steam-pressure gauge edged far above the danger point. "It seemed impossible the boilers could long stand the pressure we were crowding upon them," wrote engineer Ramsay. Outside, the shells clanged against *Merrimac*'s walls. Surely, thought the crewmen, the armored plate would have to buckle under the weight of so many hits. Finally, the men felt their ship lurch. They screamed a rebel cheer. The *Merrimac* was free!

Once in the open water, Lieutenant Jones of the *Merrimac* decided to try to ram the *Monitor*. Earlier in the battle he had dismissed the idea of ramming because he had lost his iron ram in combat the day before. "Like the wasp we could sting but once, leaving the sting in the wound," wrote engineer Ramsay. After two hours of fruitless combat, however, Jones decided to ram the other ship. He hoped the sheer weight of the *Merrimac* would sink the *Monitor*. Jones ordered full speed ahead and pointed his bow at the *Monitor*'s broadside. Like a bull, the *Merrimac* charged its enemy. But moments before the crash, the more nimble *Monitor* pivoted away. What was planned to be a ramming turned out to be a nudge.

For both captains the battle was becoming maddening. They tried every trick in their seaman's experience, but neither could damage his opponent. At one point, the tiny *Monitor* even tried to ram the huge *Merrimac.* Officers on both ships discussed plans to sail close to their enemy, have their crews jump aboard, and then fight hand-to-hand. But none of these plans could be executed. Instead, the two iron giants continued their cannon duel while thousands of spectators looked on from the shore as if they were watching two boxers in a ring.

Finally, each captain decided to concentrate his fire on what he considered to be his opponent's most vulnerable point. Worden of the *Monitor* ordered his gunners to fire at the *Merrimac*'s rudder. Jones of the *Merrimac* aimed his cannon at the tiny pilothouse that jutted abovedecks near the bow of the *Monitor.* Standing in the pilothouse were Lieutenant Worden and his wheelman.

With a terrific explosion, a *Merrimac* shell struck the eyeslit of *Monitor*'s pilothouse. Gunpowder and

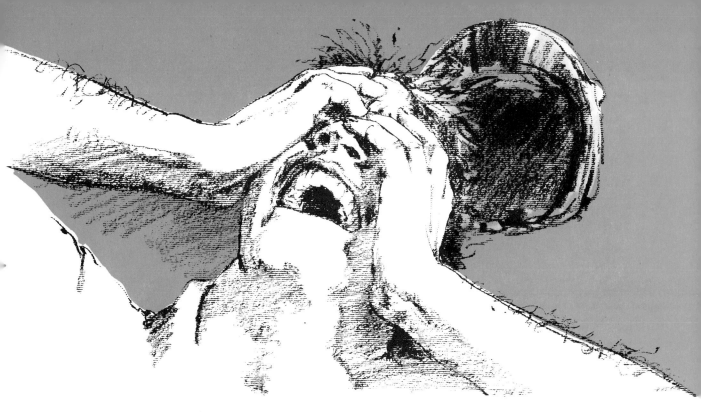

flames seared Worden's face. In agony, Worden covered his face with his hands and told a messenger to fetch Lieutenant Greene, who was next in command. Lieutenant Greene later described what he found upon entering the pilothouse: [the captain's] "face was perfectly black with powder and iron and he was perfectly blind. . . . He said a shot had struck the pilothouse exactly opposite his eyes, and blinded him. . . . He told me to take charge of the ship. . . . I led him to his room, and laid him on the sofa, and took his position."

During the change of command, the *Monitor* drifted away from the battle site. *Merrimac* sailors cheered, thinking the enemy ship was retreating.

Quickly the *Merrimac* trained her guns on the ship she had come to destroy—the wooden *Minnesota*. But during the long gun duel, the tide had fallen. Lieutenant Jones was afraid he would again run aground if he moved his ship close enough to shell the *Minnesota*. So Jones decided to steam back into the Elizabeth River. At that same time the *Monitor*, with Greene in command, hastened back to the battle site. Now the *Monitor* sailors cheered, believing the *Merrimac* was retreating. Thus the battle ended—with both sides thinking they had won.

For three hours the two iron giants had done everything in their captains' power to destroy each other. But in the end neither ship was badly damaged, and not one seaman had been killed. Even Lieutenant Worden, who had been blinded, eventually recovered his sight.

For years afterward, the North and the South argued about which side had actually won this duel of iron. The *Monitor* suffered more damage. But the *Monitor*'s orders were to protect the grounded *Minnesota*. She succeeded in protecting that vessel. The *Merrimac*'s orders were to crush the blockade that had been strangling Confederate shipping. She did not succeed in doing that.

The most lasting influence of the battle was its impact on naval planning. As one newsman wrote, [this battle] "will create a revolution in naval warfare, and hence iron will be the king of the seas." For the remainder of the Civil War, both the North and the South had crash programs to build more ironclads. The industrial North easily outbuilt the agricultural South. By the end of the war the Northern navy had commissioned thirty-one *Monitor*-type gunboats.

The first duel between ironclads touched off an iron shipbuilding program that swept the world. Never again would a nation build a major wooden warship. Suddenly all the maritime countries wanted fleets of ironclads. And they tried to build their ironclads a little bigger, a little speedier, and with more-powerful guns than their neighbors' ironclads. Soon scientists designed shells that could penetrate iron plate. Naval engineers, in turn, built ships with even thicker armor. Over the decades, guns became still more powerful and warships more massive. Finally, by the 1940s, battleships existed that were so huge that one of their turrets alone weighed almost as much as the *Monitor*.

The warships *Monitor* and *Merrimac* never again

fought each other. About two months after their historic battle, Union forces captured Norfolk, Virginia, where the *Merrimac* was based. Her crew blew up the *Merrimac* so the ship would not fall into Northern hands. Ten months after the battle, the *Monitor* sank in a gale off Cape Hatteras, North Carolina. In 1974 scientists found and photographed her encrusted hull as it rested under 220 feet of water. Perhaps salvage crews will someday be able to bring the historic ship to the surface.

The first clash between armored ships became one of history's most important sea battles. The gun duel between the *Monitor* and the *Merrimac* marked the end of an era of wood and sail, and the beginning of an era of steam and iron.

*About the Author*

**R. Conrad Stein** was born and grew up in Chicago. He enlisted in the Marine Corps at the age of eighteen, and served for three years. He then attended the University of Illinois, where he received a Bachelor's Degree in history. He later studied in Mexico and earned a Master of Fine Arts degree from the University of Guanajuato.

The study of history is Mr. Stein's hobby. Since he finds it to be an exciting subject, he tries to bring the excitement of history to his readers. He is the author of many other books, articles, and short stories written for young people.

*About the Artist*

**Keith Neely** attended the School of the Art Institute of Chicago and received a Bachelor of Fine Arts degree with honors from the Art Center College of Design, where he majored in illustration. He has worked as an art director, designer, and illustrator and has taught advertising illustration and advertising design at Biola College in La Mirada, California. Mr. Neely is currently a freelance illustrator whose work has appeared in numerous magazines, books, and advertisements. He lives with his wife and five children in Flossmoor, Illinois, a suburb of Chicago.